No A.R.

YOUR LAND
AND
MY LAND
ASIA

We Visit

CHINA

Joanne

Mattern

Mitchell Lane
PUBLISHERS
P.O. Box 196
Hockessin, Delaware 19707

YOUR LAND
AND
MY LAND
ASIA

Cambodia
China
India
Indonesia
Japan
Malaysia
North Korea
The Philippines
Singapore
South Korea

We Visit

CHINA

Mitchell Lane
PUBLISHERS

Printing   1   2   3   4   5   6   7   8   9

Asia

Library of Congress Cataloging-in-Publication Data
Mattern, Joanne, 1963-
 We visit China / by Joanne Mattern.
   pages cm — (Your land and my land. Asia)
 Includes bibliographical references and index.
 ISBN 978-1-61228-476-7 (library bound)
 1. China—Juvenile literature. I. Title.
 DS706.M3557 2014
 951—dc23
                                              2013041466
eBook ISBN: 9781612285313

PBP

Contents

Introduction 6
1 Welcome to China! 9
    Where in the World Is China? 12
    Facts at a Glance 13
2 The Land 15
3 A History of China........................... 21
4 Politics and Government..................... 27
5 Economy and Business....................... 31
6 China's People 35
7 Culture and Lifestyle 41
8 Famous People............................... 47
9 We Visit China............................... 53
Chinese Recipe: Wonton Soup 56
Chinese Craft: Red Lanterns 57
Timeline 58
Chapter Notes.................................. 59
Further Reading 60
    Books...................................... 60
    On the Internet 60
Works Consulted................................ 60
Glossary....................................... 62
Index 63

Introduction

Asia is the largest continent on planet Earth. It covers about 30 percent of Earth's land area and is home to 4.3 billion people. Presently, there are 48 countries in Asia. China is by far the largest and has the most people. It also has a rich culture that goes back thousands of years.

China is home to an amazingly diverse group of people, customs, and cultures. During its history, China has had many different governments, many of which kept the nation sheltered and separate from other parts of the world.

In the past, China and its people were a great mystery. Today, thanks to a more open government and easier ways to travel, China has opened its gates to the world. Over the past 25 years, the country has changed in many ways while still maintaining many of its traditional symbols and celebrations. Let's take a trip and visit one of the largest and most fascinating countries in the world: Your Land and My Land, China!

FYI FACT:

China is known as the People's Republic of China, or PRC, while Taiwan is known as the Republic of China, or ROC. Although Taiwan has a different government than China and is recognized as a separate country by most of the world, it is not recognized as a separate country by the Chinese government.

To use as much land as possible, farmers grow rice in terraced fields in China's mountains.

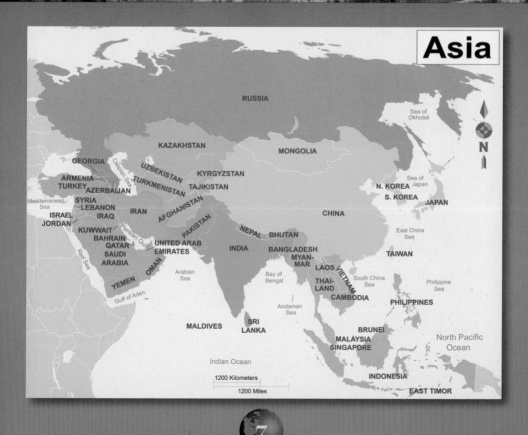

Asia

RUSSIA

Sea of Okhotsk

KAZAKHSTAN

MONGOLIA

GEORGIA

ARMENIA
TURKEY   AZERBAIJAN

UZBEKISTAN
Caspian Sea
TURKMENISTAN

KYRGYZSTAN

TAJIKISTAN

Sea of Japan

N. KOREA

S. KOREA

JAPAN

Mediterranean Sea
SYRIA
LEBANON   IRAN
ISRAEL   IRAQ
JORDAN

AFGHANISTAN

CHINA

KUWWAIT
Persian Gulf
BAHRAIN
QATAR   UNITED ARAB
SAUDI   EMIRATES
ARABIA

PAKISTAN

NEPAL   BHUTAN

INDIA   BANGLADESH
MYAN-
MAR

East China Sea

TAIWAN

Red Sea

OMAN

Arabian Sea

Bay of Bengal

LAOS
THAI-
LAND   VIETNAM

South China Sea

Philippine Sea

YEMEN

Gulf of Aden

CAMBODIA   PHILIPPINES

Andaman Sea

MALDIVES   SRI LANKA

BRUNEI
MALAYSIA
SINGAPORE

North Pacific Ocean

Indian Ocean

1200 Kilometers
1200 Miles

INDONESIA

EAST TIMOR

Shanghai's skyline includes many modern buildings, such as the oddly shaped Oriental Pearl Tower at left.

Welcome to China!

Welcome to China, one of the largest countries on Earth! There is so much to see and do in this country. Traveling through China will take you to many different places. You'll see mountains, coastal areas, and deserts, modern cities and old-fashioned farms, and many different cultures and people.

China takes up a large part of the continent of Asia. It covers 3,705,407 square miles (9,596,960 square kilometers), making it the fourth-largest country in the world after Russia, Canada, and the United States. Because China is so big, it shares borders with 14 different neighbors.

China is also one of the oldest countries in the world. It was founded more than 2,200 years ago. During most of its history, China was ruled by many different emperors. In modern times, China's government changed to rule by the Communist party. For hundreds of years, China was closed off to many other parts of the world. Today, all that has changed. People from many different countries travel to China every year, and many international companies do business there.

Mount Everest is the highest place in the world. Part of the mountain is located in China! Mount Everest is in the Himalayan Mountains. These mountains are so high that people call this area the "Roof of the World."

Another "big thing" about China is its population. China is home to more than 1.3 billion people. That means China has the largest population of any country in the world. There are many different

One of the most famous landmarks in the world is the Great Wall of China. Parts of it were built over 2,000 years ago to protect the Chinese kingdom against armies invading from the north. Until very recently, people believed that the Great Wall was about 5500 miles (8,850 kilometers) long. But according to a five-year archaeological survey completed in 2012, the length is actually 13,170 miles (21,195 kilometers).[1] The wall has steep steps and is lined with guard towers. In ancient times, guards lived in these towers and kept watch over the countryside to make sure no one came over the border to attack the country. Today, parts of the Great Wall are open to tourists. Anyone can come and walk along this ancient landmark. For many years, people believed that the Great Wall was the only human-built structure that could be seen from outer space. But even from low-earth orbit, it blends into its surroundings.[2]

Mount Everest sits on the border of China and Nepal. Every year, many people travel to the area to attempt to climb the world's highest mountain.

ethnic groups in China. Most Chinese people belong to a group called Han, but you will also find Koreans, Mongolians, Tibetans, Yao, Miao, and many other ethnic groups.

From the deserts of the north and the mountains of the west to the coastal areas of the east and south, China is a country of many different cultures. Let's pack our suitcases and get ready for the trip of a lifetime—a visit to China!

FYI FACT:

The Chinese alphabet is not made up of letters like the Western alphabet. Instead, Chinese people write in characters. Each character stands for a word or a sound. There are around 50,000 characters in the Mandarin Chinese language.

Where in the World

China is part of Asia. China shares its borders with 14 countries and three seas. It is the largest country located entirely in Asia, and the fourth-largest country in the world.

CHINA FACTS AT A GLANCE

Official Country Name: People's Republic of China

Official Language: Mandarin Chinese

Population: 1,349,585,838 (July 2012 estimate)

Land Area: 3,705,407 square miles (9,596,960 square kilometers); slightly smaller than the United States

Capital: Beijing

Government: Communist

Ethnic Makeup: Han Chinese 91.5%; Tibetan, Korean, and other 8.5%

Religions: Officially atheist, but many people are Taoist, Buddhist, Christian, or Muslim

Exports: Electrical and other machinery, apparel, telephones, textiles, integrated circuits

Imports: Electrical and other machinery, oil and mineral fuels, optical and medical equipment, metal ores, motor vehicles

Crops: Rice, wheat, corn, millet, barley, potatoes, peanuts, apples

Climate: Hot, dry summers; moderate winters

Average Temperatures:
    Beijing: August 77°F (25°C); January 25°F (-4°C)

Average Annual Rainfall:
    Beijing: 24.4 inches (62 cm)

Highest Point: Mount Everest 29,035 feet (8,850 meters)

Longest River: Yangtze 3,915 miles (6,300 kilometers)

National Flag: China's flag was adopted in September 1949. It has a red field with a large golden-yellow star in the upper left corner and a semicircle of four smaller golden-yellow stars next to the large star. The red color of the flag symbolizes revolution. The large star stands for the Communist Party and the smaller stars represent China's people.

National Sport: Officially none, but table tennis is the most popular

National Flower: Plum blossom

National Bird: Red-crowned crane

National Tree: Ginkgo

Sources: CIA World Factbook: China
Encyclopedia Britannica http://kids.britannica.com/comptons/article-195643/China
Travel Guide China http://www.travelguidechina.com

Hong Kong is one of the busiest ports in the world. Many different boats fill the city's Victoria Harbor.

2

The Land

China is an enormous country that is located in the eastern part of Asia. It is larger than the continent of Australia and almost as big as the entire continent of Europe.

Since China is so large, it has many different climates and landforms. Let's start our explorations at the tallest place in the world: Mount Everest. This mighty mountain rises 29,035 feet (8,850 meters) in the western part of China, in a mountain range called the Himalayas. The Himalayas are located on the border between China and Nepal. This area is called the Tibetan Highlands. The land is so rocky and bare that very few people live there.

Moving north of the mountains, you'll find the Zinjiang-Mongolian Uplands. This area has mountains as well as two of the driest deserts in the world. These deserts are the Gobi Desert and the Taklimakan Desert. Sand from the Gobi Desert often blows south into other parts of China, creating dusty conditions hundreds of miles away.

The central and eastern part of China is made up of plains, grasslands, and valleys. This area is called the Eastern Lowlands and has some of the best farmland in the nation. Two of China's largest and most important cities are located in the Eastern Lowlands: Beijing, which is the capital of China, and Shanghai, an important business center. Above the Eastern Lowlands is an area called the Eastern Highlands. This area has thick forests.

You can visit bamboo forests in many places in southern China. Bamboo grows tall and straight, and even though it looks like a tree, it is actually a type of grass. It is one of the fastest-growing types of plants and some kinds of bamboo can grow up to three feet in one day! Bamboo is used to make medicine, food, furniture, buildings, and even clothes. Because bamboo can live for more than a hundred years, it has become a symbol of good luck and long life in Chinese culture.

The Qinling mountain range stretches across China from the Tibetan Plateau to the Eastern Lowlands. These mountains divide the country into two specific climates. North of the mountains, the climate is dry and cool. South of the mountains, the climate is warm and humid.

The Southern Uplands cover the southwestern part of China. This area has many hills. In southeastern China, a flat area called a delta surrounds the Pearl River. This area is full of farms and also holds some of China's largest cities, such as Guangzhou, Shenzhen, and Hong Kong.

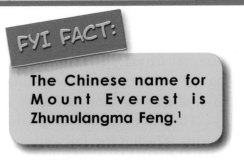

China has a large number of islands off its eastern and southeastern shores. The Zhoushan Archipelago is made up of more than 1,300 islands. Hong Kong consists of more than 200 islands. Hainan Island is one of China's largest and most important islands.

China has several major rivers. The longest and most important are the Yangtze, which is also called the Long River, and the Huanghe, or the Yellow River. The Yangtze is the third-longest river in the world. During the summer months, heavy rains often cause the Yangtze to flood. Some towns along the river have gates that can be raised to prevent it from flooding the streets.[2] In addition to rivers, China's eastern coast runs along the Yellow Sea and the East China Sea. In the south, the South China Sea surrounds the southeastern coast.

China has many different landforms, and it has many different climates too. The northern and western parts of China can have bitterly cold winters. Temperatures can drop into the teens or even lower!

The Luokou Yellow River Railway Bridge is one of many bridges that cross China's Yellow River.

Central China has temperate weather—cold in the winter and warm in the summer. Southern China has a tropical climate. It is warm and humid all year long and a lot of rain falls.

The monsoon winds are one of China's most predictable weather events. During the fall and winter, these powerful winds blow down from the north, bringing cold temperatures to many parts of China. In the spring and summer, the opposite happens. At that time, the monsoon winds blow across China from the south and bring moisture from the Indian Ocean. These winds create powerful storms that can bring days or even weeks of heavy rains. Sometimes violent storms called typhoons blow in from the ocean with especially high winds and heavy rains.

The Wolong National Nature Reserve in western China has more pandas than any other zoo or wildlife preserve in the world.

Since China has so many different landforms and climates, it also has many different animals and plants. More than 30,000 plant species live in China.[3] These plants range from the conifer, or evergreen, trees in the northern mountains, to bamboo and ginkgo trees that grow in the tropical southern areas. Other common trees in China include elms, oaks, maples, and fruit-bearing trees such as mandarin orange trees and lemon trees.

China also has thousands of animal species. There are large mammals such as tigers, snow leopards, bears, and river dolphins. Yaks live in the cold mountains, while antelope, deer, and horses race across the grasslands. Alligators also live in rivers and swamps, along with many kinds of fish. Golden monkeys and gibbons (a kind of ape) live in tropical forests in the south.

The giant panda is probably the most famous animal in China. This large mammal can weigh up to 300 pounds and spends most of its time eating bamboo. Giant pandas were once common in China's bamboo forests and mountains, but they have become rare in the wild because the bamboo forests have been cut down to create farms and cities. The Wolong National Nature Reserve in Sichuan, China, is working to save giant pandas. More than 150 pandas live in the reserve, where scientists help the animals to give birth to baby pandas so that the species can continue to survive.

Golden monkey

In 1974, some farmers digging in a field made an amazing discovery. They found more than 8,000 life-sized statues of soldiers from Qin Shihuangdi's burial site. These soldiers were made of a type of clay called terracotta, so they became known as the terracotta warriors. Qin Shihuangdi probably had the soldiers built so he would have an army to help him rule in the afterlife. The statues have many details and no two are alike. Today you can visit the terracotta warriors in the city of Xi'an.

poetry became known all over Asia. After the Tang dynasty, there was a period of military unrest. Finally, the Song dynasty began in 960. Many new cities were settled, and China's population grew to more than 100 million people. However, the country was too big for the Song emperors to rule. In 1215, an army of Mongols led by Genghis Khan swept into China from the north and eventually conquered much of the nation. Genghis Khan's grandson, Kublai Khan, became the new leader of China in 1271 and began the Yuan dynasty.

In 1369, the Mongols were forced out of China and the Ming dynasty began. During this time, China had increasing contact with Europeans. The next dynasty—which became the final one—was the Qing dynasty, which lasted from 1644 to 1912. During this time, the emperors expanded trade but also tried to keep traditional Chinese customs. The population grew to more than 400 million people by the mid-1800s. There was not enough money, food, or land for all those people. Foreign countries, such as Great Britain, Russia, Japan, France, and the United States got involved in China's affairs. In 1911, the people rebelled and got rid of the Qing dynasty.

The Republic of China was established the following year. Dr. Sun Yat-sen, leader of the Nationalist Party, became China's first president, but he could not bring peace to the new nation. After Sun Yat-sen died in 1925, his army commander, Chiang Kai-shek, took control. He wanted to have complete power over China, but other people did not like this idea.

The Communist Party fought against Chiang Kai-shek. The Communists believed that the government should own all businesses and have complete control of the economy. The Nationalists and the Communists fought many battles until Japan declared war on China in 1937. In 1939, that conflict became part of a larger war—World War II. Many parts of China were under Japanese control until the war ended in 1945. Then the Nationalists and Communists went back to fighting each other. Finally, in 1949, the Communists won. Their leader, Mao Zedong, proclaimed a new nation, the People's Republic of China, on October 1.

FYI FACT:

At first, Chinese leaders called themselves kings. This changed when Qin Shihuangdi called himself an emperor. After that, most Chinese leaders referred to themselves as emperors.

Communism changed China completely. The government took control of all businesses and industries. It also took land away from farmers. By the late 1950s, millions of people were starving because there weren't enough farms to grow food for everyone. Chairman Mao, as he was called, did not want anyone to criticize what he was doing. He especially disliked people with an education, such as writers, teachers, scientists, and politicians. These people were sent far away from home to do hard labor in the countryside. This period was called the Cultural Revolution, and it lasted for about ten years.

A huge statue of Genghis Khan looks over the central square of Ulan Bator, the capital of Mongolia.

Tiananmen Square is a large, open plaza in the capital city of Beijing. A large picture of Chairman Mao hangs on the wall. Over the years, Tiananmen Square has been the site of many public gatherings. In 1989, students gathered there to call for more freedom and a democratic government. After several weeks, army tanks rolled into the square and soldiers fired on the protesters. Hundreds of people were killed and many others were sent to prison.

Chairman Mao died in 1976, and Deng Xiaoping became China's leader. China had been almost completely cut off from the rest of the world during Mao's leadership. Deng began to change that. He allowed more economic freedom and allowed businesses to have more control over their work. Some democratic ideas came into Chinese culture and government during Deng's 21-year rule. However, China remains a communist country and the government still controls most aspects of life.

The National People's Congress gathers for its yearly meeting.

Chapter 4

Politics and Government

China has a communist government. According to communism, people should work for the good of the nation rather than themselves. Communist governments control many parts of people's lives. In a communist country, people can be told what jobs they can have or where they can live. Travel is also restricted and so are sources of news. Chinese media outlets report only what the government says they can report, and Internet access is restricted to block certain news stories. In China and other communist countries, there is little freedom of speech. Criticizing the government can land a person in jail—or worse.

China's government is divided into three parts: executive, legislative, and judicial. China's leader and the head of the executive branch is the president, but he is not elected the way the president of the United States is. Instead, China's president is chosen by leaders of the Communist Party. The president can only serve two five-year terms. However, the real power lies with the General Secretary, or the leader of the Communist Party. Sometimes one person can hold both offices.

The State Council has most of the power in China. This group oversees the many ministries, or departments, that run different parts of Chinese society. These ministries include education, finance, justice, health, and many more. Ministries create laws and policies that everyone in China has to follow.

The National People's Congress (NPC) is the legislative part of the government. The NPC has about 3,000 members, who are elected by people all over China. Each member of the NPC serves a five-year

China is one of the world's largest exporters of electronics. These factory workers are testing notebook computers before shipping them out to customers around the world.

term. Because the NPC is so large and only meets one month of the year, they do not get much business done. Instead, a smaller group called the Standing Committee meets and votes on most everyday issues.

China's judicial branch is in charge of making sure people obey the law. There are courts throughout China, and the highest court in the land is the Supreme People's Court. This court reviews decisions made by the lower courts and also tries important cases. There are more than 300 judges on the Supreme People's Court. Most of them are elected because they have ties to the Communist Party, and cases are often decided based on political interests rather than legal principles. Chinese justice can be harsh, with long prison sentences and even the death penalty for some crimes.

China is a very large country, so the executive and legislative branches cannot run everything. Instead, China is divided into different

FYI FACT:

China's national anthem is called "March of the Volunteers." It was written for a movie in 1935 and became the national anthem in 1949, when the Communists came to power.

provinces, just like the United States is divided into 50 states. Currently, China has 22 provinces. There are also five regions that govern themselves. These five regions are Tibet, Inner Mongolia, Guangxi Zhuang, Ningxia Hui, and Zinjiang Uygur. In addition, there are four municipalities, which are the highest-ranked cities in China: Beijing, Chongqing, Shanghai, and Tianjin. Finally, there are two special administrative regions, Macau and Hong Kong. In the past, Macau was ruled by Portugal and Hong Kong was controlled by Great Britain, so these areas have different rules and lifestyles than other parts of China do. For this reason, Macau and Hong Kong have been allowed to create their own governments, although they are still controlled by China.

China's constitution outlines the role of the Chinese government and what rights the Chinese people have. The constitution was created in 1982 but has been amended, or changed, many times over the years. In 1993, the constitution was amended to limit government control of economic issues. This allowed people to start their own businesses and have more opportunities in their professions. In 2004, the constitution was amended again to allow people to have more private property and other rights.

In 1997, Great Britain turned control of Hong Kong over to the Chinese, and Portugal did the same with Macau two years later. Both areas are ruled under a principle called "one country, two systems." This principle means that both Hong Kong and Macau are free to create their own laws and policies, except in the areas of national defense and foreign affairs.

A huge container ship piled high with cargo docks in Qingdao, one of China's major seaports.

Economy and Business

China's economy is one of the most powerful in the world and it seems to be getting bigger all the time. Since the 1980s, China's economy has grown at about 10 percent a year, which is the largest increase of any country in the world.[1] China is the world's largest exporter, selling more goods to other countries than any other nation.[2] In 2012, China's gross domestic product, which is the total value of all the goods and services produced, was more than eight trillion dollars.[3]

Because it is a communist country, China's government controls almost all of the nation's economy. This had disastrous consequences after the Communist Party took control of the country and all parts of its economy in 1949. China's leader, Mao Zedong, wanted to change China from an agricultural nation, in which most people lived and worked on farms, to an industrial nation, where people manufactured goods and provided services. However, so many people were forced to leave their farms and work in factories that China could not produce enough food for its people. Between 20 and 40 million people starved to death between 1958 and 1961.[4]

Mao Zedong died in 1976 and Deng Xiaoping took over the country. Deng moved away from the planned economy and allowed people to have more opportunity. He introduced some elements of a capitalist economy, where people can build their own businesses. Deng gave land back to farmers during the 1970s and 1980s to increase food production. He also allowed other countries to invest money in China.

China began building the Three Gorges Dam in 1994. Apart from a ship lift, the project was completed in 2012. The dam is located on the Yangtze River in Hubei Province and is the world's largest power station. Along with using water power to generate electricity, Three Gorges Dam also controls flooding along the Yangtze River and helps make it easier for ships to navigate on the river as well.

This policy was never practiced when Mao was in charge, because he kept China cut off from most of the world.

Deng's changes helped the Chinese economy grow stronger. Private citizens and small businesses have more freedom over their work, although the government does still control larger industries such as banking and oil. The standard of living has increased and poverty levels have dropped. However, prices have gone up as well. Also, without government controlling and supporting industries, unemployment rates rose because companies that didn't make enough money had no choice but to go out of business.

Manufacturing is big business in China. The nation is filled with factories which make just about every product on Earth. Many of these products are sold to companies around the world who are able to save money because China can produce things so cheaply. China makes products such as shoes, clothes, toys, televisions, radios, computers, cell phones, and all kinds of machinery.

China is also one of the largest producers of minerals in the world. The nation mines iron, steel, tin, nickel, tungsten, zinc, silver, and gold. China also produces large amounts of coal, oil, and natural gas.

Newly manufactured train cars sit in a Chinese factory.

Service industries are another big part of China's economy. Stores, restaurants, hotels, hair salons, real estate offices, banks, and other businesses have come to employ more than one-third of China's workforce. Many people work in tourism. At one time, traveling to China was very difficult and even impossible. During the 1990s, China began welcoming tourists from all over the world. In 2012, nearly 58 million foreign tourists came to China, making it the third most-visited country in the world. Only France and the United States attract more tourists.[5] Restaurants, hotels, tour companies, museums, and transportation companies have all added jobs to serve all those visitors.

Agriculture, or farming, was once the major part of China's economy, but today the percentage of agriculture jobs is much smaller. Even so, China is the largest producer of agricultural products in the world.[6] Its farms produce rice, wheat, potatoes, peanuts, soybeans, barley, corn, cotton, and many other products, along with chicken, eggs, and pork.

FYI FACT:

China's money, or currency, is called renminbi, which means "people's money." The basic unit of currency is the yuan. Mao Zedong's picture is on all of China's paper money.

quickly. To stop this situation from growing worse, the government established a law called the One Child Policy. This law said that families could have only one child. Any family who had more than one child could be fined. As a result, many of today's families are very small. Even though the government has relaxed this rule, it is still unusual to find a Chinese family with more than two children.

It is common for several generations of a family to live together. Sons are responsible for taking care of their elderly parents, so a household might include one or two parents, their son and his wife, and their grandchildren. Since Chinese tradition states that sons should take care of their parents, daughters usually end up taking care of their in-laws since they are part of the husband's family.

As in other cultures, men and women start families by getting married. In the past, parents chose who their children would marry. Often a matchmaker was asked to find a suitable husband or wife. However, today most young people are free to choose their husband or wife. Couples might be married in a traditional ceremony or by a government official. After the wedding, there is often a special meal or party with family and friends.

Red is a symbol of good luck in China, so many traditional Chinese brides wear red gowns. However, white gowns are becoming more popular as China has more Western influences.[2]

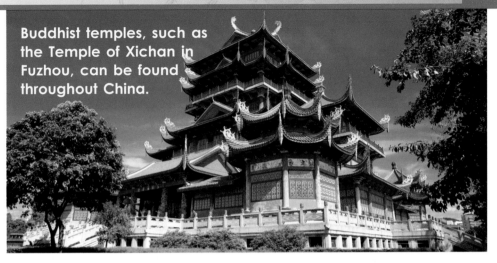

Buddhist temples, such as the Temple of Xichan in Fuzhou, can be found throughout China.

Education is very important in China. Children are under a lot of pressure to do well in school so they can get good jobs. By law, children start school when they are six years old. They go to school from 8:00AM until 5:00PM, six days a week. After six years of primary school, Chinese students go on to a six-year high school. They study many different subjects, including history, geography, literature, writing, math, science, computers, art, and music. Children also have physical exercise classes. After high school, some students take a national exam. If they do well on the test, they can go to university.

China has no official religion because the communist government does not believe in religion. However, many Chinese people follow Buddhism or Taoism. These are ancient religions that teach people to live in harmony with nature and to perform good deeds. There are many Buddhist temples all over China. People come to these temples to pray and to leave gifts, such as food. They also honor Buddha by lighting sticks of incense, which makes a sweet, smoky smell.

There is also a substantial Christian population in China, as well as a National Catholic Church. Catholics in China are not supposed

FYI FACT:

In China, a person's family name comes first and his or her given name comes second. So someone named John Smith would be called Smith John in China.

The Lion Dance is a noisy and exciting part of many Chinese New Year celebrations.

to follow the Pope, as Roman Catholics do, but instead follow Chinese religious leaders. While the exact number of Christians in China isn't known, according to an article in the British Broadcasting Corporation News Magazine, "No one denies the numbers are exploding. The government says 25 million, 18 million Protestants and six million Catholics. Independent estimates all agree this is a vast underestimate. A conservative figure is 60 million."[3]

The religion of Islam also has many believers in China. Many of the smaller ethnic groups in China are Muslims. The CIA World Factbook says that they may total between one and two percent of the total population, or between 15 and 30 million people.

As you can imagine, there are many different languages in China. There are more than 300 different languages spoken in this country. The official language is Mandarin Chinese. This is the language

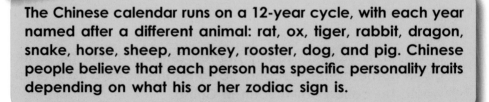

FYI FACT:

The Chinese calendar runs on a 12-year cycle, with each year named after a different animal: rat, ox, tiger, rabbit, dragon, snake, horse, sheep, monkey, rooster, dog, and pig. Chinese people believe that each person has specific personality traits depending on what his or her zodiac sign is.

FYI FACT:

One of the most beautiful and important Buddhist temples in China is the Nanshan Temple in Sanya in southern China. Nanshan Temple has many different buildings and halls built in the traditional Chinese style. These buildings have wide red roofs and white walls. The temple also has many huge statues and beautiful gardens where many people come to pray or just enjoy the scenery.

children learn when they go to school. In southern China, many people speak Cantonese, which is a different form of the Chinese language. In addition, most areas have dialects, or languages that are spoken only in those areas.

Holidays are very important in China. Perhaps the most famous and popular holiday is the Chinese New Year. The Chinese New Year falls in late January or early February, depending on the cycle of the moon. Before the Chinese New Year, everyone cleans their houses and pays back any money they owe so they can begin the new year with a fresh start.

Since red is a lucky color in China, people decorate their homes and the streets with red paper lanterns. There are also parades led by a figure of a dragon. People set off firecrackers and bang on gongs to make lots of noise to scare away evil spirits. Then families sit down to a delicious meal that usually includes uncut noodles, which symbolize long life. Children are especially lucky on New Year's because they receive special red envelopes with money inside.

The Mid-Autumn Festival is another important holiday. It usually falls in September and honors the moon goddess. To celebrate, Chinese people enjoy eating special pastries called moon cakes. Moon cakes can be filled with many different things, including dried fruit, nuts, or chocolate.

October 1 celebrates the day in 1949 that the Communist Party came to power. On and around October 1, many cities in China have special events such as parades to mark this important day in Chinese history.

FYI FACT:

Kites are another unusual Chinese art form. Children and adults enjoy making and flying beautifully painted kites. Many people think that a Chinese man named Lu Ban invented the first kite more than 2,000 years ago.[3]

Most Chinese stories have been written down. Chinese people invented paper more than 2,000 years ago. They also invented the first system of printing. In China, writing itself is an art. This art is called calligraphy. Calligraphers use special brushes to make Chinese characters that tell stories.

After the Communists took control of China, they insisted that all literature had to serve the government. That meant that stories and poems had to talk about how wonderful communism and the Chinese government were, and how bad other forms of government were. This type of writing is called propaganda. In the 1970s, the government relaxed this policy, and Chinese literature began to express different subjects. Today, there is more freedom for writers and artists, especially through online publishing. However, there is still little freedom of speech in China, and people who speak out against the government face prison and other severe punishments.

Chinese art is very beautiful and takes many different forms. Early paintings and sculptures focused on everyday subjects, such as animals, nature, and people. Later, landscape paintings became popular. Chinese art also features mythological creatures such as dragons. Sculptors often use precious stones, such as jade, to create beautiful figures.

Folk crafts are also popular in China. Chinese people enjoy paper-cutting, in which elaborate designs or pictures of animals are cut out of colored paper. These designs are often hung up in people's homes as decorations during holidays. Many Chinese children also learn to embroider, or create beautiful designs with thread on cloth.

Music is very important in Chinese life. Traditional Chinese music does not sound like Western music at all. This type of music features percussion instruments, such as gongs, bells, and drums, along with flutes and pipes, and stringed instruments such as the erhu (a fiddle with two strings) and the guqin (a stringed instrument that rests on a table or a person's lap while it is played). Over the years, Chinese music has changed and accepted many Western influences. Today, Chinese people enjoy many types of music, including pop, rock, and even Mandarin rap!

Chinese calligraphy

Soong continued to work toward fair treatment for the Chinese people. When Mao Zedong came to power, she became one of his closest aides and helped shape China's policies, including equal rights for women. Soong was named Honorary President of the People's Republic of China in 1981, just two weeks before her death. She is the only woman to ever hold this title.

The Dalai Lama
"Dalai Lama" is actually a title given to this spiritual leader. The current Dalai Lama is Tenzin Gyatso. He was born in 1935 in Tibet and educated as a monk. In 1950, the new communist government of China threatened to take over Tibet. Even though he was just a teenager, the Dalai Lama became Tibet's Head of State and Government. He met with China's leaders several times over the next few years, but in 1959, he was forced into exile in India when the Chinese army occupied Tibet. He still lives in exile and works to bring a peaceful solution to the problems between China and Tibet. In 1989, the Dalai Lama was awarded the Nobel Peace Prize for his work.

I.M. Pei
Ieoh Ming Pei is one of the most famous modern architects in the world. He was born in the southern China city of Canton (now called Guangzhou) in 1917. Because of his abilities, he left China in 1935 to study architecture at the Massachusetts Institute of Technology and Harvard University in Boston, Massachusetts. Pei's style is very abstract and features materials such as concrete, glass, and stone. Some of his most interesting and famous buildings include the Bank of China in Hong Kong, the East Wing of the National Gallery in Washington, D.C., New York City's Javits Convention Center, the Pyramide du Louvre in Paris, and the Rock and Roll Hall of Fame in Cleveland, Ohio.

Hong Kong's Bank of China shows I.M. Pei's style in its glass walls and abstract shapes.

Yue-Sai Kan

Called "the most famous woman in China,"[4] Yue-Sai Kan is an award-winning television pioneer. She was born in Guilin, China, in 1949, but grew up in Hong Kong. As a young woman, she and her sister moved to New York City, where she became involved in television work. In 1972, Yue-Sai created and hosted a weekly TV series called *Looking East* which introduced Asian cultures and customs to an American audience. The series aired for 12 years and made Yue-Sai famous as the first TV journalist to connect the East and West. In 1984, Yue-Sai hosted the first live broadcast of a television program from China, co-produced by the Public Broadcasting System (PBS) in the United States and China's CCTV network. After that, Yue-Sai became well-known in China and was offered a television series there called *One World*. It was the first time a television series was hosted by a Chinese-American on national Chinese TV and had a weekly viewership of 300 million people. Because she had television series running in both China and the United States at the same time, Yue-Sai became the most-watched woman in the world and influenced the next generation of television journalists in China. She is also known for her work in fashion design, cosmetics, publishing, and humanitarian efforts.

Yue-Sai Kan is one of the most popular broadcasters both in China and in the Asian community in the United States.

Jet Li

Fans of martial arts movies will recognize Jet Li as one of China's biggest action stars. Li Lianjie (his Chinese name) was born in Beijing in 1963. When he was eight years old, he began studying the Chinese martial art of wushu. By the age of 11 he was a national champion. Li retired from martial arts when he was 19 and began making movies. His first film, *Shaolin Temple*, came out in 1982 and made him a huge star in China. Later, Li moved to Hong Kong, which has a very active martial arts movie industry. In 1994, he made his American film debut in *Lethal Weapon 4*. He went on to star in many more English-language movies as well as movies in China.

Yao Ming

Although most people in China are short, Yao Ming towers over Chinese and Americans alike at a height of seven feet, six inches (2.29 meters). His height and athletic ability allowed him to become one of basketball's biggest stars. Yao was born in Shanghai in 1980 and began playing professional basketball in China when he was still a teenager. In 2002, he joined the Houston Rockets of the National Basketball Association (NBA) and became Rookie of the Year. He played in eight NBA All-Star Games before his retirement in 2011. In 2008, he was honored by carrying the Olympic torch into the stadium at the start of the Beijing Summer Olympic Games.

Lang Lang

One of the most famous concert pianists in the world, Lang Lang was born in Shenyang, China, in 1982. He began taking piano lessons at a young age and eventually went to Beijing to study at a famous music school there. Lang won many awards and appeared on Chinese television programs. Later, he moved to Philadelphia to study music and went on to appear in concerts all over the world. Lang has played with major orchestras and singers, and performed for government leaders from many different nations. In 2008, an estimated four billion people watched on television as he performed at the Opening Ceremony of the Beijing Olympics.

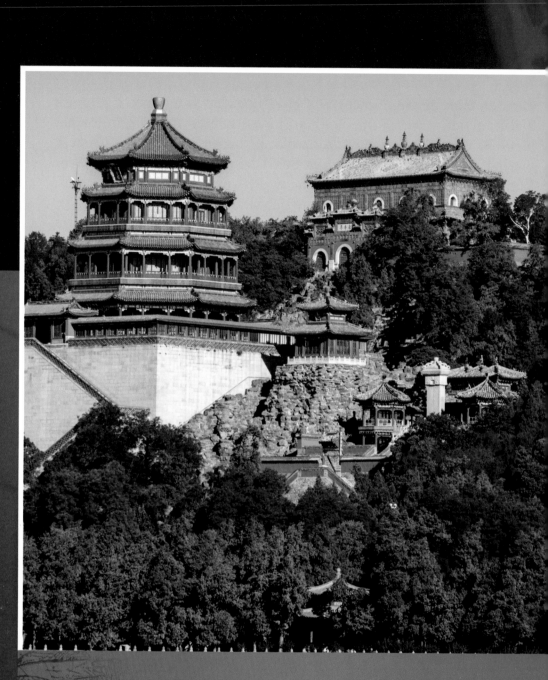

This beautiful garden is just one of the wonders in the Summer Palace. Once enjoyed only by the emperor, it is now a popular tourist spot.

We Visit China

There are many amazing places to visit in China. Some of the most beautiful and magical places are related to the emperors who ruled China long ago. If you visit China's capital city, Beijing, you will discover several places where the emperors lived, worked, and played.

The Forbidden City is one of the most famous sites in all of China. There are many palaces in Beijing, but the Forbidden City is the largest and most important. It was the home of the Chinese emperors for 500 years. Built between 1406 and 1420, the palace includes 980 buildings and more than 8,700 rooms. Twenty-four different emperors and their families lived there until Puyi, China's final emperor, was driven out of the palace in 1924.

The palace was called the Forbidden City because at one time, anyone who was not part of the emperor's family was forbidden to enter it and the emperor and his family were forbidden to leave. Today the Forbidden City contains the largest group of ancient wooden buildings in the world. It is open to the public so everyone can marvel at the place where China's royal family lived.

Since summers can be hot and uncomfortable in Beijing, the emperor and his family needed to find a cooler place to stay for those hot months of the year. The answer was to move to the Summer Palace, just over nine miles away from central Beijing. Workers began building the palace in 1750 and it served as a retreat until 1924. At that time, the last Chinese emperor was forced out of the palace and the Summer

FYI FACT:

> If you visit the Forbidden City, you will see a lot of yellow tiles, yellow bricks, and yellow paint. That's because yellow was the color of the royal family.

Palace was opened to the public. It is the largest and best-preserved royal park in China.

The Summer Palace is filled with many beautiful things. Gardens filled with a variety of flowers cover the grounds. The walls and walkways are made of beautifully painted tiles and there are more than 3,000 ancient buildings, including pavilions, towers, and bridges. There is also a large lake called Kunming Lake where visitors can ride boats and marvel at a huge boat made of marble that was built by Empress Cixi in the late 1800s.

Visitors to Beijing have a lot to see and do, but a visit to the royal palaces should delight anyone who loves history, artwork, or just a glimpse into a life very different from our own. The Forbidden City and the Summer Palace are just a small part of the land that is China.

A bronze lion stands guard inside the Forbidden City.

Wonton Soup

This soup is popular in China and all over the world. The soup is a rich broth filled with wontons, which are small dumplings filled with pork.

Ingredients:
8 ounces ground pork
1 tablespoon finely chopped scallions
1 egg, beaten
1 tablespoon soy sauce
1 tablespoon sugar
1 tablespoon water
1 package wonton wrappers (24 per package)
4 cups chicken or vegetable broth

Instructions:
Prepare the following recipe with adult supervision:
1. Mix pork, scallions, egg, soy sauce, sugar, and water.
2. Lay out wonton wrappers. Put one teaspoon of the pork mixture in the center of each wrapper. Wet your fingers and fold wontons into triangles, pressing the edges together to seal in the filling.
3. Bring a large pot of water to a boil. With the help of an adult, drop in a few wontons at a time. Cook over medium heat for 10 minutes. The wontons will float to the top when they are cooked.
4. In a separate pot, bring broth to a boil.
5. Transfer the cooked wontons to the broth with a slotted spoon. Cook for one more minute.
6. Pour soup into bowls and serve. Serves 4 people.

Red Lanterns

Red is a lucky color in China, and you will often see red lanterns hanging up for decorations, especially during New Year's celebrations. Here's how to make your own red lantern.

Materials
- Red construction paper
- Pencil
- Scissors
- Stapler, tape, or glue

Instructions
1. Fold a piece of construction paper in half to make a long rectangle.
2. Draw a line about one inch from the unfolded edge.
3. Cut slits all along the paper along the fold line, about half an inch apart. Cut up to the line you drew in step #2, making sure not to cut all the way through the paper.
4. Unfold the paper and glue, staple, or tape the short edges together to make your lantern.
5. Cut another strip of paper 6 inches long by half an inch wide. Glue, staple, or tape the strip across the top of the lantern to make a handle.

FURTHER READING

Books

Catel, Patrick. *China*. Chicago: Heinemann Library, 2012.

Goh Sui Noi and Lim Bee Ling. *China*. Welcome to My Country Series. New York: Marshall Cavendish Benchmark, 2011.

Mara, Wil. *People's Republic of China*. Enchantment of the World Series. New York: Children's Press, 2012.

Mattern, Joanne. *Recipe and Craft Guide to China*. Hockessin, Delaware: Mitchell Lane Publishers, 2011.

On the Internet

China: Enchanted Learning.com
 http://www.enchantedlearning.com/asia/china/
China Facts and Pictures: National Geographic Kids
 http://kids.nationalgeographic.com/kids/places/find/china/
China: Time for Kids
 http://www.timeforkids.com/destination/china
Chinese Zodiac: 12 Animal Signs
 http://www.travelchinaguide.com/intro/social_customs/zodiac/
Fun China Facts for Kids
 http://www.sciencekids.co.nz/sciencefacts/countries/china.html
Learn Mandarin
 http://www.tuvy.com/chinese/learn/learn_mandarin.htm

WORKS CONSULTED

Abbey, Jennifer. "Great Wall of China Longer Than Previously Reported." ABC News, July 18, 2012. http://abcnews.go.com/blogs/headlines/2012/07/great-wall-of-china-longer-than-previously-reported/

Atkinson, Nancy. "Can You See the Great Wall of China from Space?" Universe Today, June 5, 2013. http://www.universetoday.com/25364/can-you-see-the-great-wall-of-china-from-space/

Beijing Summer Palace
 http://www.travelchinaguide.com/cityguides/beijing/summer.htm

Branigan, Tanya. "China's Great Famine: The True Story." *The Guardian*, January 1, 2013. http://www.theguardian.com/world/2013/jan/01/china-great-famine-book-tombstone

China Facts, China Flag: *National Geographic*
  http://travel.nationalgeographic.com/travel/countries/china-facts/
China's Top Ten Temples and Monasteries
  http://www.chinahighlights.com/travelguide/temples-and-monasteries/
China: 2,000 Years of Cooking
  http://www.globalgourmet.com/destinations/china/#axzz2gEyYWRcl
CIA World Factbook: China
  https://www.cia.gov/library/publications/the-world-factbook/geos/ch.html
"China: Crops and Livestock." Encyclopedia Britannica Kids
  http://kids.britannica.com/comptons/article-195643/China
"Facts About China." Maps of World.
  http://www.mapsofworld.com/china/china-facts.html
"Forbidden City—Beijing Palace Museum," Travel China Guide
  http://www.travelchinaguide.com/cityguides/beijing/forbidden.htm
"The 14th Dalai Lama—Biographical," Nobelprize.org
  http://www.nobelprize.org/nobel_prizes/peace/laureates/1989/lama-bio.html
Gardam, Tim. "Christians in China: Is the country is spiritual crisis?"
  BBC News Magazine, September 11, 2011. http://www.bbc.co.uk/news/
  magazine-14838749
Jet Li Biography
  http://www.biography.com/people/jet-li-241077
List of Countries in Asia
  http://www.countries-of-the-world.com/countries-of-asia.html
Mah, Adeline Yen. *China: Land of Dragons and Emperors*. New York: Delacorte
  Press, 2009.
"I.M. Pei," Great Buildings Online
  http://www.greatbuildings.com/architects/I._M._Pei.html
Profile of Soong Ching-Ling
  http://people.brandeis.edu/~dwilliam/profiles/ching-ling.htm
Reed, Susan. "Helping East Meet West Via TV, America's Yue-Sai Kan Has
  Become the Most Famous Woman in China." *People*, May 18, 1987.
  http://www.people.com/people/archive/article/0,,20096315,00.html
Short Bio: Yue-Sai Kan
  http://www.yuesaikan.com/short-bio.html
"Soong Ching-Ling (1893-1981)." Women Leaders and Transformation in
  Developing Countries, Brandeis University. http://people.brandeis.
  edu/~dwilliam/profiles/ching-ling.htm
Spence, Jonathan. Mao Zedong. *Time*, April 13, 1998. http://content.time.com/
  time/magazine/article/0,9171,988161,00.html
Travel Guide China
  http://www.travelguidechina.com
Uschan, Michael V. *China Since World War II*. Detroit: Lucent Books, 2009.

architects (AHR-kih-tekts)—People who design buildings.

atheist (AA-thee-ist)—Someone who does not believe in God.

calligraphy (kah-LIG-ruh-fee)—The art of painting written symbols.

communist (KOM-yoo-nuhst)—A person who supports communism, a political system in which the entire community owns all property equally.

constitution (kon-stuh-TOO-shuhn)—A document containing the laws of a country, including the rights of the people and the powers of the government.

corruption (kuh-RUP-shuhn)—Dishonest activity, often used in reference to government officials.

delta (DEL-tuh)—A flat, often triangular-shaped area of fertile land near the mouth of a river where it empties into the ocean.

democratic (dem-uh-KRAT-ik)—A type of government in which everyone has equal rights.

dynasty (DYE-nuh-stee)—A line of rulers belonging to the same family.

emperors (EM-per-urs)—Male rulers of an empire.

ethnic (ETH-nik)—Relating to a group that shares a common culture or heritage.

invest (in-VEST)—To put money into a business.

martial arts (MAR-shuhl ARTS)—Styles of fighting or self-defense that come from the Far East.

merchants (MER-chuntz)—People who buy goods from those who make them and then sell those goods to the public.

monk (MUNK)—A man who lives in a religious community and devotes his life to prayer and meditation.

monsoons (MAHN-soonz)—Regular, predictable seasons of heavy rain.

philosophy (fuh-LOSS-uh-fee)—The study of truth and wisdom.

republic (ree-PUB-lik)—A country where political power lies with the people.

revolution (reh-vuh-LOO-shuhn)—A violent uprising by the people against the government.

rural (RUR-uhl)—Having to do with life in the country.

typhoons (ty-FOONZ)—Violent tropical storms.

urban (UHR-buhn)—Having to do with life in the city.

Western (WEST-uhrn)—Relating to countries in the Western part of the world, such as the United States, South America, and Europe.

animals   19

art   42

Asia   6, 9, 15, 21, 22

bamboo forest   16

Beijing   15, 25, 29, 41, 51, 53–54

Buddhism   37, 39

calendar   38

calligraphy   42

Catholics   37–38

Chiang Kai-shek   23

Chinese New Year   39

Christians   37–38

climate   15, 17–19

communism   24, 25, 27–28, 42

Communist Party   23, 27, 31, 39

Confucius   47

constitution   29

Cultural Revolution   24

Dalai Lama   48

Deng Xiaoping   25, 31

dragons   41

drama   41

dynasties   21–23

economy   31–33

education   37

emperors   9

family life   35–36

folk crafts   42

Forbidden City   53–54

Genghis Khan   22

government   27–31

Great Wall of China   10

Han   11, 35

Himalayas   9

holidays   39

Hong Kong   16, 29

I.M. Pei   48

Islam   38

islands   17

Japan   6, 37

Jet Li   50

kites   41, 42

Kublai Khan   22

landforms   15–17

Lang Lang   51

languages   38–39

Lu Ban   42

Macau   29

Mao Zedong   23–25, 31, 32, 48

Mid-Autumn Festival   39

Mongols   22–23

monsoons   18

moon cakes   39

Mount Everest   9

music   43

myths   41

Nanshan Temple   39

National Art Museum of China   41

National Catholic Church   37

National People's Congress (NPC)   27–28

Nationalist Party   23

One Child Policy   36

opera   44

pandas   19

plants   19

population   9, 35

provinces   29

Qin Shihuangdi   22

religion   37

Republic of China   23

rivers   17

Shanghai   15, 29, 51

Silk Road   21

Soong Ching-Ling   47–48

sports   44–45

State Council   27

Summer Olympic Games   51

Summer Palace   53–54

Sun Yat-sen, Dr.   23, 47

Supreme People's Court   28

tai chi   44

Taoism   37

terracotta warriors   22

Three Gorges Dam   32

Tiananmen Square   25

Tibet   48

tourism   33

typhoons   18

Wolong National Nature Reserve   19

World War II   23

Yangtze River   17, 32

Yao Ming   51

Yellow River   17

Yue-Sai Kan   50

Joanne Mattern is the proud mother of four children who were adopted from China. During her trips to China, she fell in love with the country's rich history, culture, and traditions. Joanne is the author of many books for children on a variety of subjects including history, biography, and nature. She has written many biographies for Mitchell Lane, as well as several books about China's food and culture. Joanne lives in New York State with her husband, children, and several pets.